Anthony Robinson writes children's books and teaches. He has lived and travelled all over the world, from his original home in Australia to Siberia. He now lives in Cambridge. In his writing he is committed to giving a voice to the voiceless, be they refugees who have fled their own countries, children living normal lives in vastly different cultures, or children living in difficult circumstances. He is the author of the Refugee Diaries series for Frances Lincoln Children's Books: *Gervelie's Journey, Hamzat's Journey, Mohammed's Journey* and *Meltem's Journey*.

June Allan was born in Edinburgh. She has illustrated many children's books, including the Refugee Diaries series with Anthony Robinson, as well as *Encore Grace* and *Bravo Grace*, with Mary Hoffman. She lives in Edinburgh with her husband and two children.

**This book is dedicated to street children wherever they are in the world.
It is written to acknowledge their lives and listen to their voices, so often unheard.**

Thanks
My gratitude goes first to all the children who spoke
to me and shared their thoughts and feelings with me.

To write this book I needed a great deal of help and
received it from many people, too many to mention here –
I have thanked many of them personally.

My special thanks go to:
Street Child Africa, a UK-based charity,
and their partners, Meniños de Mozambique:
www.streetchildafrica.org.uk

Streets Ahead in Zimbabwe: www.streetsahead.org

Camino Seguro (Safe Passage), who helped me in Guatemala:
www.safepassage.org

**I would like to thank the Society of Authors for their generous support
of this project with a grant from the Authors' Foundation.**

JANETTA OTTER-BARRY BOOKS

Text and photographs copyright © Anthony Robinson 2014
Illustrations copyright © June Allan 2014

First published in Great Britain and in the USA in 2014 by
Frances Lincoln Children's Books,
74-77 White Lion Street,
London N1 9PF
www.franceslincoln.com

This paperback edition first published in Great Britain in 2015

A catalogue record for this book is available from the British Library.

ISBN 978-1-84780-598-0

Printed in China

1 3 5 7 9 8 6 4 2

Real Stories from
STREET CHILDREN
Across the World

Anthony Robinson
With Photographs by the Author

Illustrations by June Allan

Frances Lincoln
Children's Books

Introduction

This book is about street children. Some of them, known as street-living children, live entirely on the streets, alone or in small groups. Others, known as street-working children, spend most of their time on the streets trying to survive, but return home from time to time. There are also children who live on the streets with their families.

The reasons the children are on the streets are not always simple. They include poverty, family breakdown, war, the death of parents, or physical violence within the family.

There are street children all over the world, but the children you will meet in this book are from Mozambique and Zimbabwe in Africa and from Guatemala in Central America.

In their own voices, the children talk about how they came onto the street, what their lives are like and what their hopes are for the future. Some of these children have now come off the streets. They explain why and how this happened.

As you read, you might think, 'Well, this or that situation would not have sent me to live on the streets,' but life is never that simple. The truth of these children's lives sometimes lies buried or is too painful. Sometimes they have simply forgotten.

Anthony Robinson

Street-living Children
Zimbabwe

Chippo

I am nine years old. I come from Rusape, a small place in the south of Zimbabwe.

My mum died when I was two and my dad was killed by a thief a month later. It was a bad time for me. Granny took me and my sister away then. Soon, my sister went away. I don't know where.

Then a man came, a relation of Granny's.
I don't know who he was. He said he wanted
me to go to school and he brought me to Harare
on the bus. I became his slave. I had to do all his
housework. It was too much, so I ran away.

I was nine and I went alone into the city.

I was afraid and lonely. Everything around
me was so big. I found some other kids
and we stayed together. We got a bit of food,
and begged in town. Sleeping was the worst.
It's scary sleeping outside.

Then, one day, a kind lady stopped me in the street. She said, "You are too young to be on the street." She took me to a welfare office and they rang a charity called Streets Ahead. They got me into this safe house.

Me with my house mother, Theresa, and two friends

I want to go back to live with my granny in Rusape. It's OK here, better than the streets, but I want a home.

I just want a family. And school. I would love to go to school. I hope my granny can take me back. I know she has problems with money, but maybe Streets Ahead can help with that. I don't know.

Zimbabwe

Wellington

I am 12. I was born in Hwang, near the Zambian border, a long way from Harare, the capital city of Zimbabwe.

My mum ran away when I was two. My dad worked near the airport, outside Harare. So my granny took me in, but she didn't have enough food for me. I went to my dad in Harare when I was ten.

I soon ran away because Dad didn't do anything for me. I went alone onto the streets. I was there for nearly two years. Sometimes my dad came looking for me and took me home. But I just ran away again.

On the street I begged for food and money. I slept in Harare Gardens, along with some other people. The police came a lot, but we just ran away and then came back. It was good in the gardens. We used to make fires and cook stuff. Sometimes bigger guys made us give them money to sleep there.

I got hit by a car in the city about a month ago. I was begging and I didn't look. I have injuries to my head and back and I can't see properly. And I can't remember where my dad lives.

But I'm getting better here in the Streets Ahead Centre. I'm finished with the street.

When I'm better, Streets Ahead will help me find my dad. If I can't, I can go back with Granny. The Centre said they will help with money for food. Anyway, I will soon have a home. My own home, with Dad or Granny. That's so good.

When I came here to the Centre, my life was not good. I asked for help and got it. My life will change.

Guatemala

Elizabeth

I am 12. I come from Guatemala City. I never met my father. I lived with my mother for six years, but then she just left me in the street.

My gran found me and looked after me for about four years, but she got too old and sick. I was sent to a charity home here in Antigua. But they closed, so I went to a hostel.

I hated it. They used to beat us for no reason. But it wasn't all bad. I learned to sing and play the harp there.

But, in the end, it got so bad there that
I came here to our shelter, behind the market.

Every day I go and beg. We get cheap food
from the market and we cook together here.
Oh, and I've found a public shower
I can use every day. That's nice.

Our only problems are with the police.
Our two dogs bark when the police
are coming and we run off. They are
God's helpers.

God knows we are homeless
and he looks after us.

This is my life now, and my family...
but I want a real life one day. I've sung
in clubs a few times here. That's my
dream, to sing professionally one day.

Mozambique

Santos

I was born here in Maputo, the capital city of Mozambique. I am 12 or 13, I'm not sure. I used to live with my mum, dad, big sister and brothers. But my mum didn't like me, so she left.

Then my big sister got married and left. I was at school in those days. And one day when I got home, I found out my older brother had had a fight with my dad and left home. I was ten.

Then my dad got another wife and stopped working. I don't know why. My little brother and me started going onto the streets and begging. We needed to eat.

My gran found out and came and took my little brother to live with her. Dad was angry all the time and would beat me a lot, even if I did everything he asked me to do.

One day I fought back. That was it, really. So I left. I was 11.

Now I come to the Meniños Day Centre every day to meet my friends. We leave in the afternoon and beg at the *robots* (traffic lights) for money or food. We play in the park if we have made money for dinner, and then sleep downtown in the parks.

When I grow up I want to be an engineer or a government minister.

Street-working Children
Mozambique

Denio

I am Denio Adriano Bernard and I am 12 years old. I was born in Quelimane in the north of our country, Mozambique.

My family came to Maputo from Quelimane when I was very young. My dad was looking for work. Then my parents split up. I went back to Quelimane with my dad. Then he remarried, and his new wife didn't want me.

So I came back to Maputo to be with my mum. But she was with another man. She didn't want me either. And anyway, this other man treated me like a dog. He would lock me out of the house at night and not give me food.

That's when I left home. I was almost ten. I went straight to the central market. I got some work sweeping up, carrying things. Stuff like that.

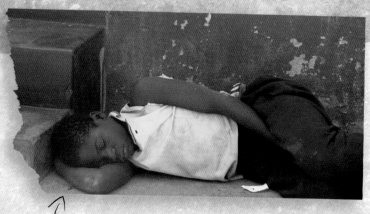

I still work the market a bit and sleep there sometimes with my friends, but not as much.

One of my friends

I have friends on the street. My best friend is called Helton. We look out for each other. We stay with his gran a lot, when the street gets too difficult. She is nice, but very poor, and she can't really look after us.

I like this life. I don't suffer like I did at home. I worked round the market full-time for about a year. Now Helton and me work the *robots*, begging for food and money.

About a year ago we moved in with Gran for a while. We were getting bullied by bigger kids. They would throw sandbags on us while we were asleep. And if they found any money on us, they would take it.

In our free time, we play in a big park near here. I keep my stuff there too, in a secret place.

I still don't want to go home for good, but we sleep at Gran's when we need to. I still have my freedom.

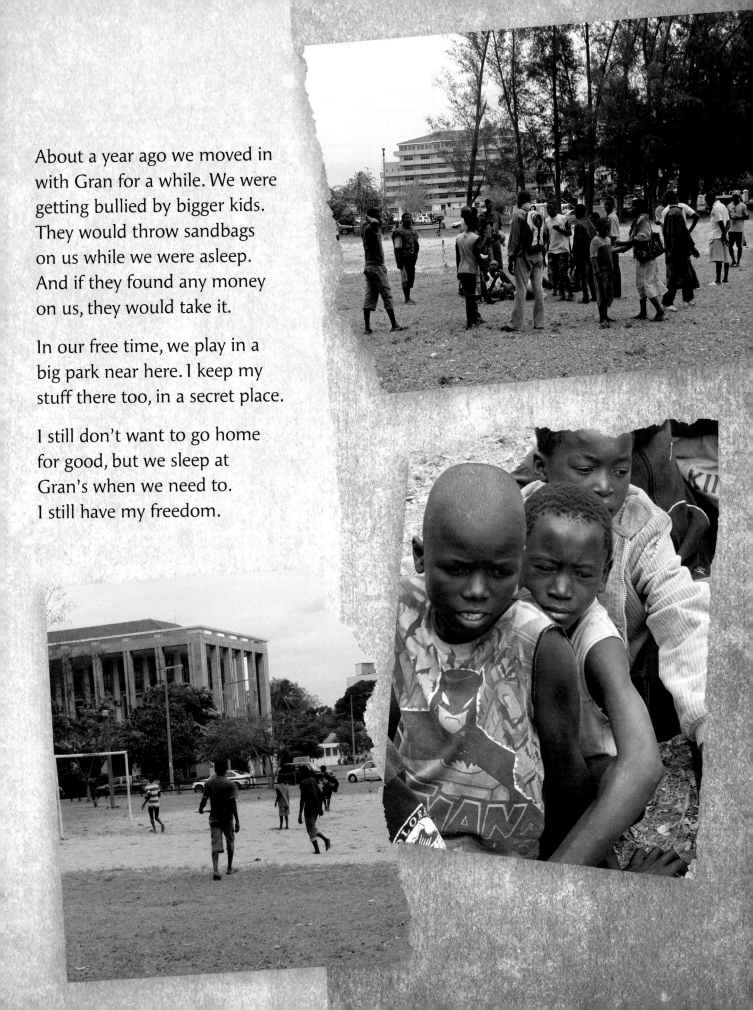

Mozambique

Miguel

I am 13. I have been working on the streets in Maputo and Benfica for about three years.

I come to the Meniños Day Centre almost every day to see my friends.

I loved my dad a lot. But he died when I was nine. We spent a lot of time together. We used to go to drinking clubs together and he would buy me alcohol.

Just after my dad died, I stole a bicycle and sold it
to buy alcohol. I was scared then that I would get
into big trouble for stealing, so I ran away to Maputo.

It was good at first. I worked every day in the market.
It was fun. I knew everybody. But everything has changed.
The people are all different now. I'm not important any more.

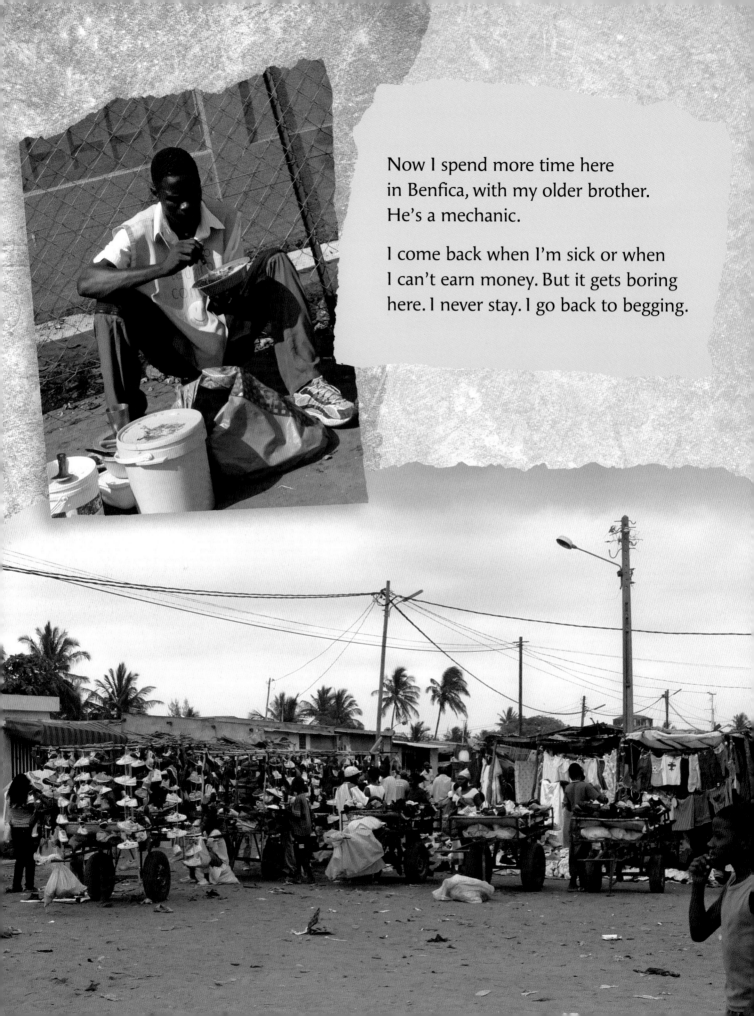

Now I spend more time here
in Benfica, with my older brother.
He's a mechanic.

I come back when I'm sick or when
I can't earn money. But it gets boring
here. I never stay. I go back to begging.

I'm with my brother now because I'm sick.
Maybe I'll stay. I don't know. I need some shoes.
I had a bad car accident on the streets a year ago
and smashed both my legs and one arm.

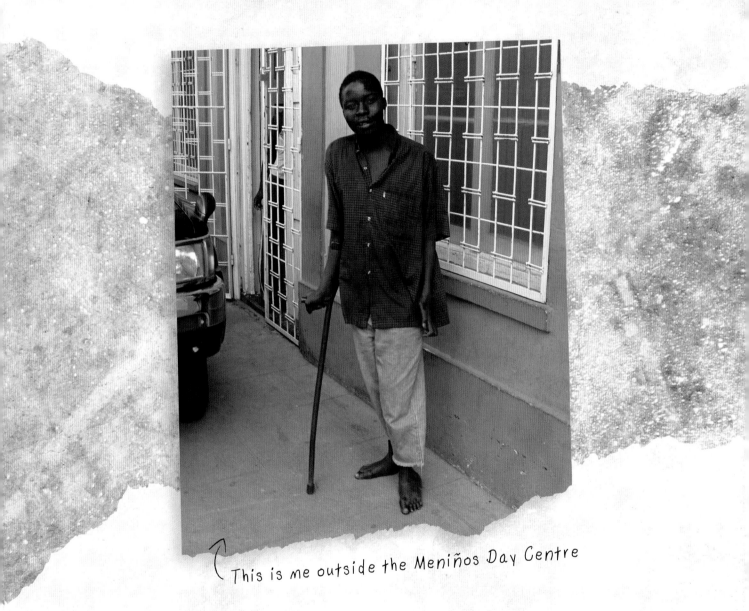

This is me outside the Meniños Day Centre

Walking is difficult. I also lost an eye. I don't know how
that happened. Recently I had TB. I don't feel strong.
I'll stay with my brother for a while. We'll see.

For my future, I want to be happy, with a family – that's all.

A Street-living Family
Guatemala

Ana Elizabeth

I am 11. We used to live in Guatemala City. My dad was very violent so we left.

Me with my mum, Maria Theresa, my sister Evelyn, little brother Joshua, and our cousin Jonathan

My mum found a house in the country. We look after it for the city people who own it. We get to live in the house, but we have to pay for electricity and water. We have no money, so we beg.

We sleep on the street most of the week and go home at weekends. I don't like begging.

I prefer the days when I stay home and go to school, because I can see my best friend Lydia. I love reading and writing. I love stories. I pretend I am in them.

I help at home every day. I clean the house, make the beds and do some cooking. My favourite food is eggs, rice and beans.

I want to be a secretary when I grow up, but I need to go to school more. I don't miss my dad.

My sister, Evelyn, is seven. She loves school. Learning is good for her. Evelyn wants to be a secretary when she grows up.

Sleeping on the streets is scary. Mum tries to stay awake, but it's still bad until the sun comes up. But what can we do?

A Street-living Family Escapes the Streets

Ingrid and family – Guatemala City

Ingrid

I am 32 and a widow. My husband, Sergio, was robbed
and murdered nine years ago. I miss him.
Three of my four children were born on the streets:
Guillermo, Christian and Brenda. We slept at
the main market and under buildings.

I was pregnant with Valerie, my youngest, when Sergio was killed. She has never known the streets and never will. We are not going back there. Never.

I borrowed money to start a business. Now I rent a room for us. I sell flags and tourist trinkets in the main square, round the Presidential Palace. I mostly make enough.

I could have lost everything on the streets, but I found treasure.

Christian

I am 16. Apart from the day my dad died,
the strongest thing I remember
from the streets, a scary thing,
was opening my eyes one night and
seeing a man standing over us saying,
"These are my children."

My dad woke up and beat the man up. I was scared.
I don't want that life again. Living under buildings
and hiding from the police. We were never safe.

We have our own room now. We are safe.
I am very proud of my mother.

I like my life now. I go to a school in the morning.
It's about skills for finding a job, and in the afternoon
I go to the Safe Passage Outreach School.
We have a free cinema near us. I love films.

I want to be a journalist.

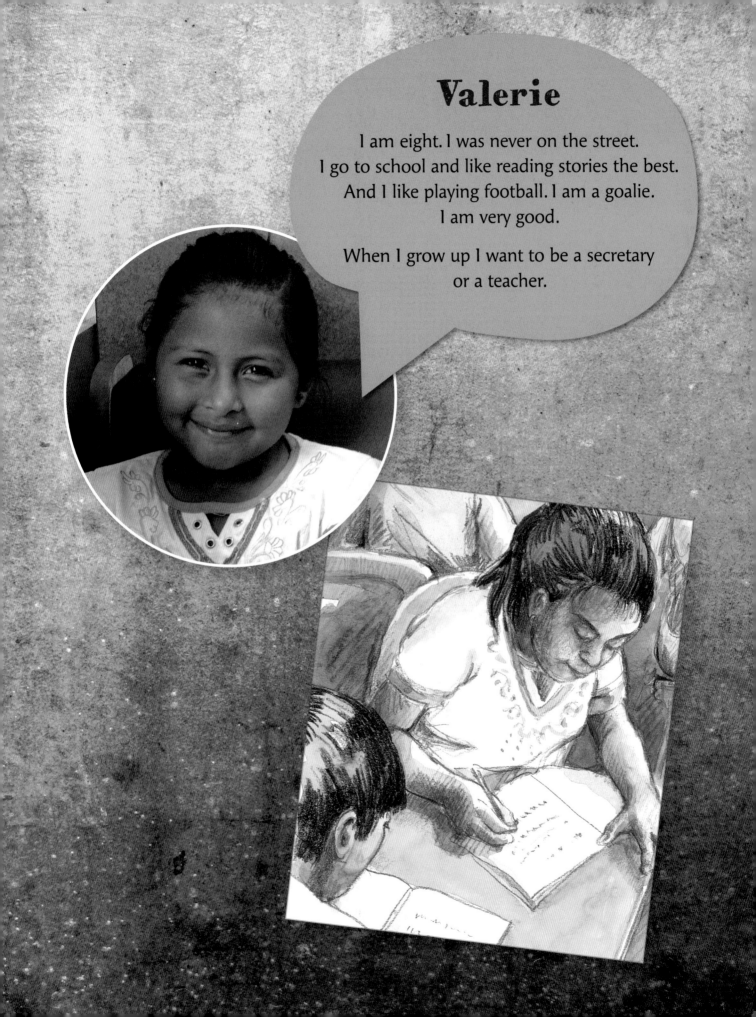

Valerie

I am eight. I was never on the street.
I go to school and like reading stories the best.
And I like playing football. I am a goalie.
I am very good.

When I grow up I want to be a secretary
or a teacher.

Street Children Around the World

How many are there?

It is hard to know exactly how many street children there are in the world, but it is thought that there are between 100 and 150 million worldwide.

Where are they?

Street children can be found all over the world, particularly in cities. The countries named on the map below and in the accompanying chart have been chosen to give a rough idea of the numbers of street children worldwide. The figures have been supplied by UNICEF.

It's important to remember that the figures are not exact, and they are always changing; and for some countries, such as Mozambique, information is simply not available.

There are also no reliable figures available for Great Britain, Australia and China. This does not mean that there are no street children in those countries. It is a fact that wherever there are vulnerable children or children at risk, some will be forced onto the streets.

Key to Map

Numbers of Street Children by country (figures supplied by UNICEF [2004-2008])

- Brazil: 7 million–8 million
- Congo: 250,000
- Egypt: 1.5 million
- Ethiopia: 100,000
- Guatemala: 7,000–10,000
- India: 11 million
- Indonesia: 170,000
- Kenya: 300,000
- Mexico: 1 million
- Mozambique: figures not available
- Pakistan: 1.2 million
- Peru: 250,000–300,000
- Philippines: 1.5 million
- Poland: 15,000–20,000
- Romania: 5,000–7,000
- The Russian Federation: 100,000–130,000
- USA: 0.75 million to 1.1 million
- Zimbabwe: 12,000–15,000

A Better Life

This book is about children in difficult, sometimes life-threatening, situations. It is, I hope, a book that shows their toughness, resilience and optimism, as well as their dreams for the things we take for granted: love and hope; a voice and a place to grow. Above all it shows the children's hopes for a future.

ALSO PUBLISHED BY FRANCES LINCOLN CHILDREN'S BOOKS

THE REFUGEE DIARIES SERIES
By Anthony Robinson, illustrated By June Allan

"Simply told and beautifully illustrated … they will act as a springboard and provide stimulus for discussion on the plight of refugees throughout the world." – *School Librarian*

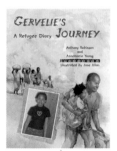

978-1-84780-004-6

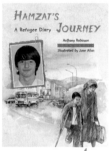

978-1-84780-030-5

978-1-84780-209-5

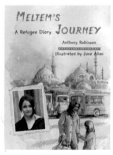

978-1-84780-031-2

GERVELIE'S JOURNEY

The true story of Gervelie's flight from the fighting in the Republic of Congo and her family's struggle to seek asylum in Britain.

Chosen by USBBY as an Outstanding International Book

Chosen as one of Scholastic's Best Books of the Year

HAMZAT'S JOURNEY

The true story of a child landmine victim from Chechnya. This poignant story reveals the bravery of Hamzat and his family in facing and overcoming their circumstances to start a new life in the UK.

MOHAMMED'S JOURNEY

The true story of an Iraqi-Kurdish refugee child, and his flight with his mother from their home in Kirkuk, travelling by bus, on horseback and in a small boat before finally arriving in the UK in a lorry.

MELTEM'S JOURNEY

13-year-old Meltem and her Kurdish family from Eastern Turkey journey to the UK and spend harrowing months waiting to find out if they can stay in Britain. Eventually the family's courage and resilience lead them to a new home and a new life.

Frances Lincoln titles are available from all good bookshops.
You can also buy books and find out more about your favourite titles,
authors and illustrators on our website: www.franceslincoln.com